The BEGINNER'S GUIDE to
ANIMAL AUTOPSY

The HANDS-IN approach to ZOOLOGY

Written by
STEVE PARKER
Illustrated by
ROB SHONE

COPPER BEECH BOOKS
BROOKFIELD, CONNECTICUT

Produced by
NW Books for
Aladdin Books Ltd
28 Percy Street
London W1P 0LD

First published in the United States
in 1997 by
Copper Beech Books,
an imprint of
The Millbrook Press
2 Old New Milford Road
Brookfield, Connecticut 06804

Editor
Simon Beecroft
Illustrator
Rob Shone
Design
David West Children's Book Design

Library of Congress
Cataloging-in-Publication Data
Parker, Steve.
The beginner's guide to animal
autopsy: a "hands-in" approach to
zoology, the world of creatures and
what's inside them / Steve Parker :
illustrated by Rob Shone.
p. cm.
Includes index.
Summary: Investigates the internal
workings of animals, with drawings
of dissections and cartoons illustrating
how the animals' bodies work, including
chapters on invertebrates, insects, fish,
amphibians, birds, and mammals.
ISBN 0-7613-0702-8 (lib. bdg.). —
ISBN 0-7613-0627-7 (pbk.)
1. Anatomy—Juvenile literature. 2. Dissection—Juvenile
literature. [1. Anatomy. 2. Dissection.]
I. Shone, Rob, ill. II. Title.
QL806.5.P37 1997   97-10032
571.3'1—dc21   CIP AC
5 4 3 2 1

4 INTRODUCTION
6 BASIC PARTS OF ANIMALS

8 Chapter One
SLITHERY-SLIMIES

10
CORAL AND JELLYFISH

11
STARFISH

12
SQUID

13
LOBSTER

14 Chapter Two
BEASTLY BUGS

16
DRAGONFLY

17
BEETLE

18
MOTH

19
BEE

20
SCORPION

21
CENTIPEDE

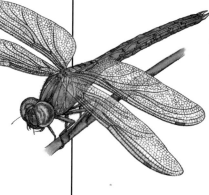

CONTENTS

22 Chapter Three
FINS AND SCALES

24
SHARK

25
SALMON

26
ELECTRIC EEL

27
FROG

28
TURTLE

29
CROCODILE

30
CHAMELEON

31
PYTHON

32 Chapter Four
FEATHERED FRIENDS

34
OSTRICH

35
PENGUIN

36
SWALLOW

37
OWL

38 Chapter Five
MAMMALS

40
WHALE

41
KANGAROO

42
BAT

43
ELEPHANT

44
TIGER

45
MONKEY

46
ANIMAL CLASSIFICATION

47
GLOSSARY

48
INDEX

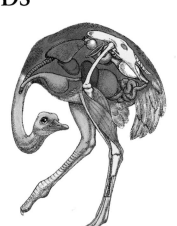
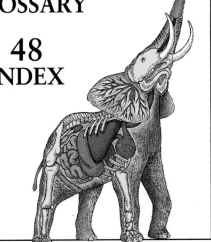

INTRODUCTION

To FIND OUT HOW A CAR WORKS, we take it apart and study its insides. If the car is broken, we replace the old parts with new ones and put it back together. Vroom!

To find out how an animal works, we take it...er, no we don't. We look in this book! There's no need to look inside a real animal. It's been done, lots of times. For hundreds of years, experts have been delving into the interiors of creatures for many reasons, including:

• **Food** Which animals were good to eat? Which pieces tasted best? Which parts would you give your enemies, because they are poisonous?

• **Understanding nature** Zoologists study how animals work, how they have evolved through the ages, and how they are related to each other.

• **Scientific knowledge about the great questions of the universe** Such as how life began, how we can change genes, how brains think, how there might be aliens out there, and how sheep can be so stupid.

• **Helping animals** A veterinarian treats a sick patient by knowing what might be wrong with its insides.

• **Helping humans** Many lifesaving medical drugs and surgical operations were developed using animals as "guinea pigs."

EXPERTS NOW KNOW A HUGE AMOUNT ABOUT creatures, their insides, and how they work. It's mainly due to animal autopsy – taking apart a creature after it dies, in a careful and scientific way, looking and learning, studying and understanding.

Animal autopsy causes no suffering or pain. And it increases our understanding of nature, evolution, the chemistry of living bodies, our pets, farm livestock, veterinary care, medicine...and ourselves.

OLD TO NEW

Olden times *People found out about animal interiors using swords, saws, scissors, and small, sharp-bladed knives called scalpels.*

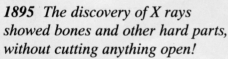

1670s *A new invention, the microscope, revealed the world of cells and other tiny body parts.*

1895 *The discovery of X rays showed bones and other hard parts, without cutting anything open!*

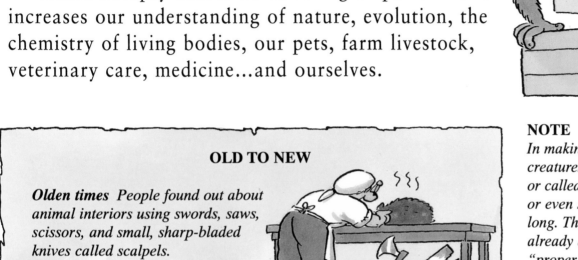

BOO!

1960s *The first medical scanners showed the detailed insides of people and animals, too – After all, there are CAT and PET scans!*

NOTE
In making this book, no creatures were harmed, or called horrible names, or even stared at for too long. The information is already available in "proper" biology books. We've portrayed our subjects as cuddly toys, furry models, and plastic kits, to make looking inside them less gory – and more fun!

BASIC PARTS OF ANIMALS

A REALLY HUGE ANIMAL, like a fat and flabby hippo, has lots of main parts inside. These are called organs. There are eyes in the head, muscles all over the body, a skeleton, breathing tubes, guts, a heart, blood, kidneys and many others, plus the most important organ of all – the brain.

A really tiny animal, like a buzzing and irritating mosquito, is about one million times smaller than a hippo. Yet inside its tiny body, which is almost too small to see, it has much the same organs. This is because animals of all different shapes and sizes have basic life processes in common. The main features of an animal, the sort of things that make it different from a plant, or a rock, or a television, are:

- Sensing the surroundings
- Reacting to them by moving
- Eating food (or taking in nourishment somehow)
- Excreting (removing body wastes)
- Growing from baby to adult
- Reproducing (making more animals)

LET'S COMPARE...
A MOSQUITO AND A HIPPO

1 THE BRAIN controls and coordinates all body processes.

2 BREATHING TUBES take in life-giving oxygen from the air.
The mosquito has breathing tubes called tracheae that open at holes called spiracles along its body.
The hippo breathes through its mouth and nose, taking air into its trachea and lungs.

3 PUMPING HEART and FLOWING BLOOD spread oxygen and nutrients around the body.

4 MUSCLES make the body move.
The mosquito's tiny flight muscles flap its wings 800 times a second.
The hippo's huge limb muscles make its legs stride once each second.

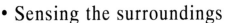
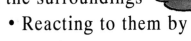
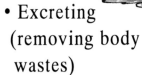

6

Cell *The smallest living unit of any plant or animal. Most cells are so small that they are only visible under a microscope.*

Tissue *Lots of similar cells. Thousands of muscle cells make up muscle tissue. Millions of nerve cells make up brain tissue.*

Organ *Main part or piece of the body. Each organ does an important job. For example, the intestine (or gut) absorbs nutrients from digested food. The liver changes these nutrients into substances the body can use.*

System *Several organs that work together to carry out one of life's basic processes. The breathing system gets oxygen from the air. The reproductive system makes more animals.*

ATTENTION!
Animal parts and insides are not always what they seem.

For example, the wings of a lacewing, seagull, and bat all look similar on the outside. They do the same job – flying. But inside, they are made of very different body parts.

7

5

7

7

2

3

8

4

1

6

4 3 8

5

6

5 SKELETONS give a supporting framework. *The **mosquito** has an outer skeleton, called an exoskeleton, which forms a hard body casing.*
*The **hippo** has an internal skeleton of bones, called an endoskeleton.*

6 EYES and OTHER SENSE ORGANS gather information about surroundings. *The **mosquito** has feelers (antennae) that detect wind and smells. The **hippo** has a tongue that tastes food to make sure it is safe.*

7 KIDNEYS filter wastes from blood and body fluids.

8 GUTS break down food into nutrients for energy and growth. *The **hippo** munches on soft plants and swallows them into its huge stomach. The **mosquito** pierces the skin of its victim with needlelike mouth-parts and sucks up blood.*

Similarly, the "feathers" of a peacock worm, the gills of a crayfish, and the lungs of a lungfish all look extremely different, yet they all do the same job – obtain oxygen from their surroundings.

CHAPTER ONE

THE ANIMAL KINGDOM is divided into two great groups, vertebrates and invertebrates. Vertebrates are animals with backbones. These are fish, amphibians, reptiles, birds, and mammals. They are shown later in the book. Invertebrates are animals without backbones. These range from jellyfish, worms, crabs, and starfish, to insects, spiders, and octopuses. They are shown over the next 14 pages. Of all animals, invertebrates have the simplest ways of feeding, taking in oxygen, and sensing their surroundings.

SADDLE

The saddle, or clitellum, is a raised section that makes lots of mucus or slime. When two worms mate, they slide and writhe around in the stuff!

MUSCLES

Each segment has two muscle layers. In the outer, or circular, layer, muscle fibers go around the body. In the longitudinal layer, they go along the body. These muscles make the worm wriggle.

THE WORM'S HEART

A worm has 10 hearts! There are five pairs of them in segments 7 to 11. Each one is just a bulge in the transverse blood vessel, which links the upper and lower main vessels. The hearts pulse gently, making the blood ooze slowly along.

EARTHWORM

8

SLITHERY-SLIMIES

BRAIN
Yes, a worm has a brain – just about. It's a thickened part of the main nerve that runs along the lower body. It wraps around the front of the gut. So the worm eats food through the middle of its brain!

HEADS OR TAILS?
Which end is which? The "head" is nearer the saddle, with its mouth, where food goes in. There are a few tiny, simple "eyes" that detect light levels. Apart from that, both ends are much the same!

HEARTS

MOUTH
A worm is basically an eating tube. Food comes into the mouth and passes through the various parts of the gut. Worms consume almost anything as they eat their way through soil.

GIZZARD
This tough, thick-walled, muscular part of the gut crushes and grinds the food into a soft paste, so it can be digested more easily by the next part, the very long intestine.

BLOOD VESSELS
A worm has two main blood tubes. Blood flows forward in the upper, dorsal, vessel, then through the hearts, and backward in the lower, ventral, vessel.

CHAPTER CONTENTS

CORAL AND JELLYFISH
PAGE 10

STARFISH
PAGE 11

SQUID
PAGE 12

LOBSTER
PAGE 13

9

PARTS OF AN EARTHWORM
What makes a worm? Segments. Lots of them, in a row, like beads on a necklace. A segment is a part or section of an animal body that is copied or repeated many times. Each one has the same parts inside, although these usually vary slightly, depending on their position along the animal.

CORAL

LOOK CLOSELY AT A CORAL REEF during the day. It seems stone dead. Look at night, and you will see thousands of tiny, jellylike creatures wave their tentacles. They are animals called coral polyps. Each one is hardly bigger than a rice grain. They catch even tinier creatures for food.

TENTACLES
These have microscopic stinging cells that paralyze and poison the polyp's prey.

MOUTH
Food enters the stomach here, in the middle of the tentacle ring. After it has been digested, the leftovers come out the same way. So the mouth is also the anus!

STALK
The main body of the polyp contains the bag-shaped stomach, with flaplike parts called mesenteries around and below. Its base anchors it to the rock.

10

JELLYFISH

THERE'S NO NEED FOR AN AUTOPSY ON A jellyfish. You can see inside. The body is called a bell – which is just what the creature looks like! Jellyfish grow from polyps, and can be as small as a pea or larger than a person. Jellyfish and corals belong to the animal group called cnidarians.

BELL
A simple network of nerves and muscle fibers make this pulse gently. So the jellyfish does not always go with the flow. It can swim against a slow current.

MOUTH

STOMACH
Strong digestive chemicals attack and dissolve the food, allowing the nutrients to spread throughout the jellyfish's body.

TENTACLES
Microscopic stinging cells paralyze small fish, shrimps, squid, and similar prey. Then the trailing tentacles pull the stunned prey into the mouth.

STARFISH

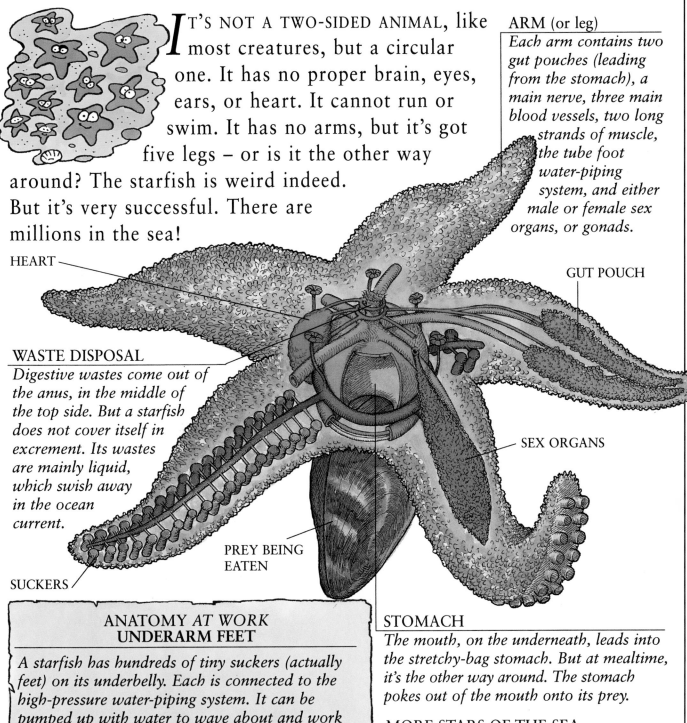

*I*T'S NOT A TWO-SIDED ANIMAL, like most creatures, but a circular one. It has no proper brain, eyes, ears, or heart. It cannot run or swim. It has no arms, but it's got five legs – or is it the other way around? The starfish is weird indeed. But it's very successful. There are millions in the sea!

ARM (or leg)

Each arm contains two gut pouches (leading from the stomach), a main nerve, three main blood vessels, two long strands of muscle, the tube foot water-piping system, and either male or female sex organs, or gonads.

HEART

GUT POUCH

11

WASTE DISPOSAL

Digestive wastes come out of the anus, in the middle of the top side. But a starfish does not cover itself in excrement. Its wastes are mainly liquid, which swish away in the ocean current.

SEX ORGANS

PREY BEING EATEN

SUCKERS

ANATOMY *AT WORK*
UNDERARM FEET

A starfish has hundreds of tiny suckers (actually feet) on its underbelly. Each is connected to the high-pressure water-piping system. It can be pumped up with water to wave about and work like a tiny sucker. Using the tube feet in wavelike relays, the starfish glides across the seabed.

STOMACH

The mouth, on the underneath, leads into the stretchy-bag stomach. But at mealtime, it's the other way around. The stomach pokes out of the mouth onto its prey.

MORE STARS OF THE SEA

Starfish are members of the animal group called echinoderms ("spiny-skins"). So are the similar sea stars and cushion stars, spiky, ball-shaped sea urchins, sausage-shaped sea cucumbers, and flower-shaped sea lilies found on the seabed.

SQUID

W HAT DO THE FOLLOWING animals have in common? Land snails, pond snails, sea snails like whelks and peri-winkles, cone shells, slugs, oysters, clams, scallops, and mussels. They're all mollusks! They're also called "shellfish" because their fleshy, flexible bodies are protected by a hard shell. Except, that is, for this one – the squid.

SHELL
The squid's need for speed means a heavy shell would just hold it back. Instead, there's a thin, light shell (called a pen) inside the body. Washed up on the shore after death, it looks like clear plastic.

INK SAC
If a predator comes near, the squid can squirt a dark-colored liquid from its ink sac, out of its anus. This clouds the water and hides the squid – with luck, just long enough to make a quick getaway.

STOMACH

LIVER

HEARTS

GILLS

BRAIN

EYES
Big enough to see you with! The squid and its close relations, octopus and cuttlefish, rarely bump into things. They have large eyes and excellent sight, for spotting prey, enemies, or a breeding partner.

BEAKLIKE MOUTH

SUCKERS

12

ARMS
There are two long arms and eight shorter ones, with suckers for grabbing prey. This is torn up by the beaklike mouth in the middle of the arm bases.

ANATOMY *AT WORK*
SQUIRT POWER
A mollusk's body is wrapped in a cloaklike, fleshy part, called the mantle. Between this and the main body is a mantle space. A squid sucks water slowly through a large opening into the mantle space, then squirts it out through a small funnel opening, and water streams away – backward.

LOBSTER

LIMBS ARE VERY IMPORTANT. They can help some animals, walk, run, flap, kick, grab, push, pull, even breathe! The huge animal group called arthropods get their name from their "jointed legs." They include lobsters and other crustaceans, shown here, as well as insects, spiders, and centipedes. (See pages 14-21.)

(See pages 14-21.)

CRUSTACEAN COUSINS
The big and varied crustacean group includes crabs, prawns, shrimps, crayfish, krill, barnacles, water fleas, and sand hoppers. The only ones that live on land are wood lice (sow bugs). Even they need damp places, to keep their breathing gills moist. A dry crustacean is a dead crustacean!

ANATOMY *AT WORK* SHEDDING THE SHELL

Arthropods have a hard outer body casing or "shell," the exoskeleton. This can't expand as the creature grows. So it's shed, or molted. The old casing splits along the back, and the animal crawls out and quickly enlarges in its soft new casing, before this hardens.

13

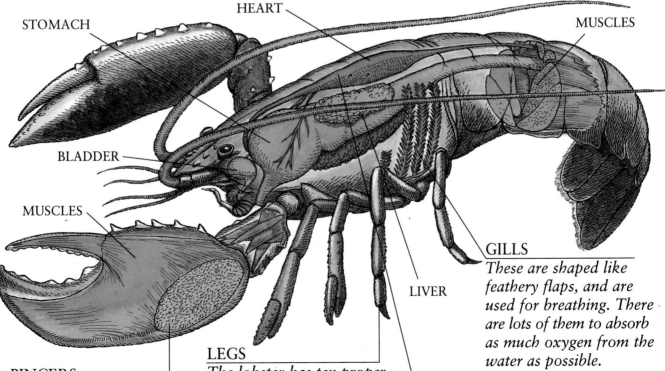

STOMACH

HEART

MUSCLES

BLADDER

MUSCLES

GILLS
These are shaped like feathery flaps, and are used for breathing. There are lots of them to absorb as much oxygen from the water as possible.

LIVER

PINCERS
The big pincer is mainly for crushing food, while the smaller, sharper one is for cutting.

LEGS
The lobster has ten proper jointed legs. But the first two are its big pincers. The other eight have claws on the end, to grip slippery seabed rocks.

BLOOD
The lobster's well-developed blood system has a powerful heart and lots of vessels. And its blood is blue!

CHAPTER TWO

Not all bugs are beastly. Blowflies, bloodsucking bedbugs, and book lice are. But butterflies are beautiful, bees are beneficial, beetles are bumbling – if a bit boring. All these creepy-crawlies have one thing in common – they are insects. This is the biggest animal group, with more than one million different kinds, or species. On the outside, insects vary incredibly in color, shape, and size, from longer than this page to smaller than this period. But their insides are very similar, as shown by this housefly.

14

WINGS
Most insects have wings. Some, like flies, have one pair. Others, like butterflies and locusts, have two pairs.

LEGS
Legs that bend at purpose-designed joints show that insects, along with spiders, centipedes, and crustaceans, belong to the main arthropod group.

GUTS
The narrow tube of the foregut leads into a big digesting organ, the midgut. The body gets its nutrients from here.

VACUUM-CLEANER MOUTH
The housefly regurgitates its own spit and digestive juices onto the food, then sucks up the soupy results with its spongy mouth, called a proboscis.

FLY EYE
Most insects see well with their big eyes. They are made of hundreds of smaller eyes (called ommatidia). Each ommatidium sees only a tiny, simple image. But added together, like a mosaic, they produce a detailed overall picture.

BEASTLY BUGS

HOLES IN THE HEART
The heart is a long, thickened section of the main blood vessel, which runs along the upper body. Blood oozes into it through holes, called ostia.

BODY CASING
The insect's squishy insides are protected by a hard outer casing, the cuticle. Like our own skeleton of bones on the inside, it provides shape, support, and attachments for muscles. Since it's on the outside, it's an exoskeleton ("exo" means outer).

THE INSECT KIT
A fully-grown insect has these main features. But newly-hatched young insects, called larvae, may not have them. The larva of the housefly, called a maggot, has none!

THREE BODY SECTIONS
The head has the mouth, eyes, and antennae (feelers). The thorax bears the legs and wings. The abdomen contains the guts and reproductive parts.

SIX LEGS
There are three pairs of legs, each made of about five jointed sections.

CHAPTER
CONTENTS

DRAGONFLY
PAGE 16

BEETLE
PAGE 17

MOTH
PAGE 18

BEE
PAGE 19

SCORPION
PAGE 20

CENTIPEDE
PAGE 21

15

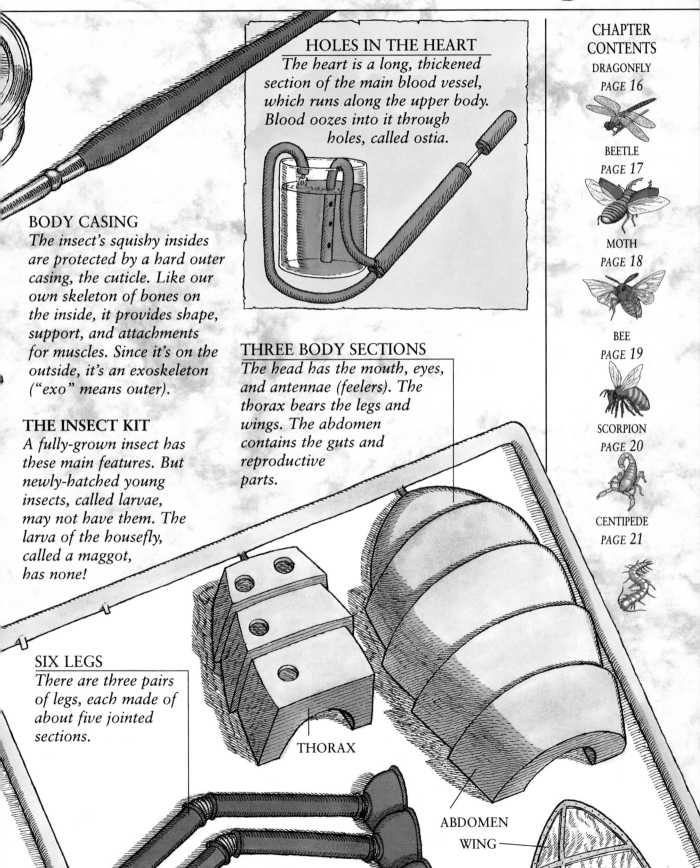

THORAX

ABDOMEN

WING

DRAGONFLY

*I*F YOU COULD GO BACK IN TIME, before the dinosaurs – 300 million years ago – then dragonflies would be the biggest flying creatures. They were the first large insects to appear on Earth. Some were the size of crows. They haven't changed much since, except to become smaller. Dragonflies are fierce hunters that catch small insects in midair.

ABDOMEN
Inside the long, thin abdomen are the usual insect innards of blood vessel along the top, guts in the middle, and main nerve along the bottom.

BREATHING TUBES

GUT

HEART

WINGS
The two pairs of see-through wings are held out sideways when resting.

EYES
Dragonflies have better eyes than all other insects. Each has more than 30,000 units, ommatidia, for incredible vision. A dragonfly can catch a tiny gnat in twilight (when we could barely see a tree).

FLYING MUSCLES

LEGS
In flight, the legs hang down to form a prey-catching "basket." Their sharp tips grip leaves or twigs when resting.

ANATOMY *AT WORK*
HOW FLIES FLY

The wings are joined to the rigid-cased thorax. This contains two sets of flight muscles. One set pulls the top of the thorax, which clicks down and flips the wings up (1). The other muscle set pulls the thorax in, making it thinner, so the top clicks back up again, flipping the wings down (2).

1

2

THE
F L Y
CLUB

NO IMPOSTERS

WHY AM I NOT A FLY?
Many insects called "flies" are not. True flies, like houseflies, bluebottles, crane flies, fruit flies, mosquitoes, gnats, and midges, have two wings. Pretend "flies," like dragonflies, damselflies, mayflies, stoneflies, and butterflies have four wings.

16

BEETLE

SOME BEETLES ARE SO TOUGH that even after you step on them they run away unharmed. This is because what looks like the beetle's abdomen (rear body part) is really a pair of wings. These have become hard and strong, like a shield, to protect the body.

FLY ON FIRE!
Fireflies are not on fire, nor are they flies. Glow worms are not worms. They are both types of beetles that glow and flash at night. Usually the female, who is wingless, makes the light – to attract a male, who flies in to mate.

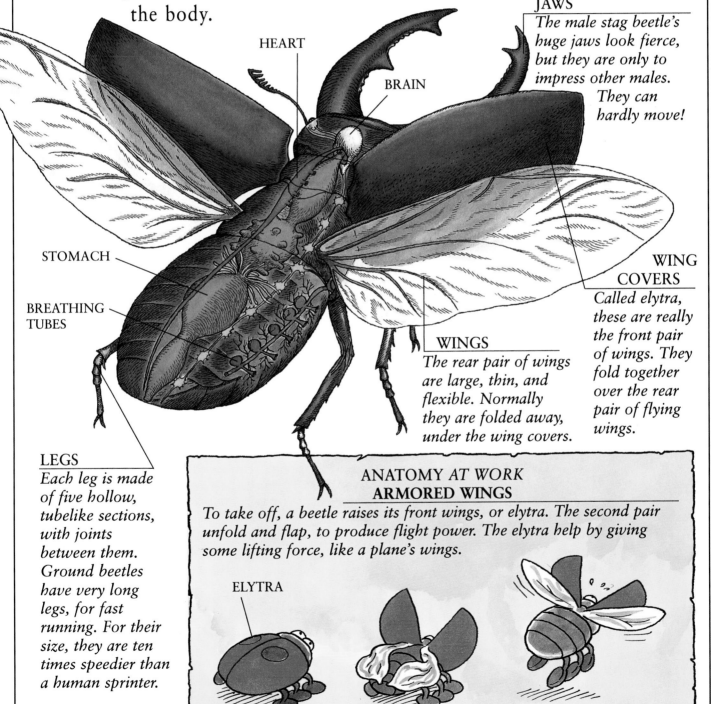

HEART

BRAIN

JAWS
The male stag beetle's huge jaws look fierce, but they are only to impress other males. They can hardly move!

STOMACH

BREATHING TUBES

WING COVERS
Called elytra, these are really the front pair of wings. They fold together over the rear pair of flying wings.

WINGS
The rear pair of wings are large, thin, and flexible. Normally they are folded away, under the wing covers.

LEGS
Each leg is made of five hollow, tubelike sections, with joints between them. Ground beetles have very long legs, for fast running. For their size, they are ten times speedier than a human sprinter.

**ANATOMY *AT WORK*
ARMORED WINGS**
To take off, a beetle raises its front wings, or elytra. The second pair unfold and flap, to produce flight power. The elytra help by giving some lifting force, like a plane's wings.

ELYTRA

17

MOTH

MOST MOTHS HAVE HAIRY BODIES, feathery antennae, wings held out sideways at rest, and fly at night. Most butterflies have smooth bodies, thin, club-tipped antennae, wings held together over the back at rest, and fly by day. But there are exceptions to all of these features. And, on the inside, moths and butterflies are almost exactly the same.

WING SCALES
The wings are covered by thousands of tiny scales, as small as dust particles. Their hues and arrangement form the wing's color and pattern.

BRAIN

ANTENNA

SEE-THROUGH WING

HEART

PROBOSCIS
This is a long tube, like a drinking straw, for sucking up sweet, juicy nectar from flowers. When not being used, it's rolled up in a spiral under the head.

STOMACH

MAIN NERVE

STORED FOR LATER
Just-sipped nectar goes into the balloonlike, stretchy foregut. This works as a storage bag, so the moth can feed quickly at a plentiful food supply and digest it later.

INTO THE BODY
Food is digested, or broken down into smaller and smaller particles, in the midgut. These seep into fingerlike pouches, called cecae, and, through them, into the blood and body tissues.

ANATOMY AT WORK
IT WAS DIFFERENT WHEN I WAS YOUNG

A tiny egg (1) hatches into a worm-shaped caterpillar, or larva (2), that eats and eats. This turns into a hard-cased chrysalis, or pupa (3), that does nothing – on the outside, at least. Inside, its body changes shape, or metamorphoses, into the adult. This crawls out of the case (4), and flies away (5).

BEE

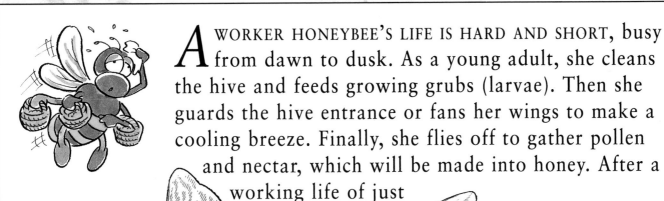

A WORKER HONEYBEE'S LIFE IS HARD AND SHORT, busy from dawn to dusk. As a young adult, she cleans the hive and feeds growing grubs (larvae). Then she guards the hive entrance or fans her wings to make a cooling breeze. Finally, she flies off to gather pollen and nectar, which will be made into honey. After a working life of just four weeks, she dies.

ANTENNAE
The antennae detect temperature, wind, and air movements, humidity (moisture in the air), smells and scents, and gravity's downward pull. They also taste chemicals and can be used to touch things.

BRAIN
A bee's brain is smaller than a pinhead. Most of it deals with information coming from the eyes and antennae – which is why bees don't think much!

HONEY FOREGUT
The bee swallows nectar and pollen into the "honey stomach," where it is turned into honey. Back at the hive, she regurgitates (brings up) most of the honey into the honeycomb's storage cells.

HEARTS

POISON GLAND

SENSORY HAIRS
Tiny bristles all over the cuticle have sensitive nerves inside them. They respond when the bristle is bent – by touch, and even by the slightest breath of wind.

FLYING MUSCLES

POLLEN BASKET ON LEG

ANATOMY *AT WORK*
SUICIDE STING
The bee's sting is in a pouch inside her rear abdomen. She contracts muscles to poke it out, then jabs it into the victim. As she flies away, the sting stays stuck in. So the sting, its pumping poison bag, and her whole rear abdomen fall off. She dies within minutes.

19

SCORPION

A SCORPION HAS TEN JOINTED LIMBS, but only eight legs. These are the rearmost four pairs, for walking. The front pair are for waving and snapping at prey or enemies. Animals with eight jointed legs are arachnids. They include scorpions, spiders, and harvestmen.

STING
The last body section, the telson, is better known as the sting. Inside it is a baglike venom gland. In some scorpions, it produces enough poison to kill a human.

STING

HEART

BODY CASING
Like insects, arachnids have a hard outer casing, or exoskeleton, made of chitin. It gives strength and support, and protects the soft insides.

LEGS
Arachnid legs are hollow tubes linked together, with muscles inside. Each leg has seven sections, not – like insects – five.

20

STOMACH

PINCERS
The large pincers are known as pedipalps. They are used for show, to scare enemies, to grab prey, and to grasp a mate at breeding time.

MUSCLES

"JAWS"
The scorpion's chelicerae are small and powerful pincers for tearing up food. In spiders, the equivalent parts are sharp, poison-injecting fangs.

BOOK LUNG

PECTINE

FEATHERY FEELERS
Under the rear body part, or abdomen, are a pair of comblike pectines. They gently brush the ground and detect vibrations.

ANATOMY *AT* WORK
BREATHING BY THE BOOK

Spiders and scorpions have a bodywide network of breathing tubes, like insects. Also, in a lower body chamber, they have book lungs. These have many flaps, like the pages of a book, to give a large surface area for absorbing as much oxygen as possible.

CENTIPEDE

"*CENTI-PEDE*" MEANS "100-FEET," but hardly any centipedes have exactly this number. Many types have 30, while a few have more than 300. Centipedes are nighttime hunters of small animals like worms, insects, and their close relatives, millipedes.

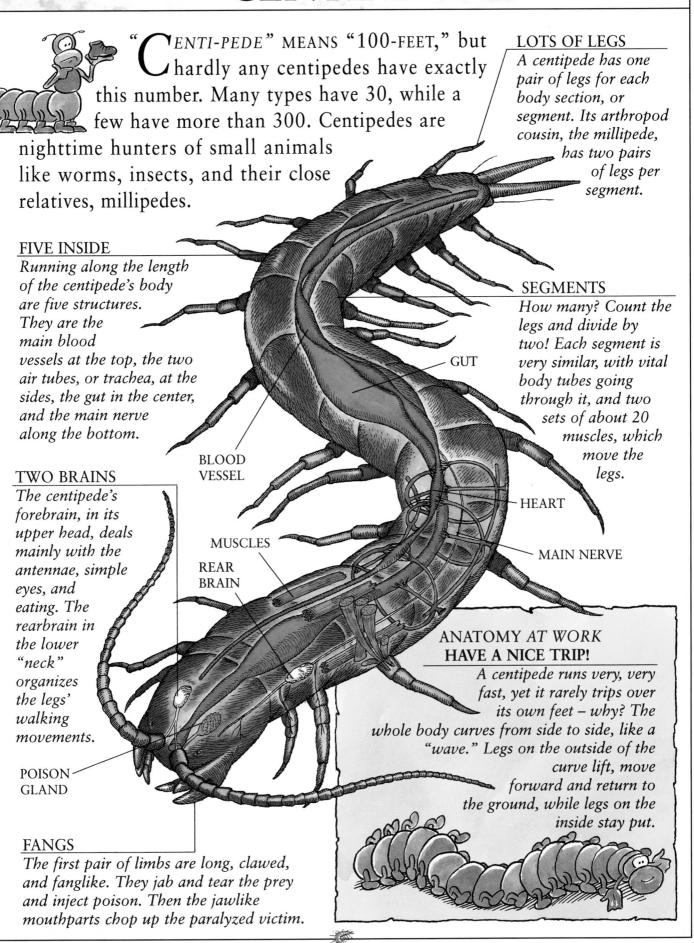

LOTS OF LEGS
A centipede has one pair of legs for each body section, or segment. Its arthropod cousin, the millipede, has two pairs of legs per segment.

FIVE INSIDE
Running along the length of the centipede's body are five structures. They are the main blood vessels at the top, the two air tubes, or trachea, at the sides, the gut in the center, and the main nerve along the bottom.

SEGMENTS
How many? Count the legs and divide by two! Each segment is very similar, with vital body tubes going through it, and two sets of about 20 muscles, which move the legs.

GUT

BLOOD VESSEL

HEART

MAIN NERVE

TWO BRAINS
The centipede's forebrain, in its upper head, deals mainly with the antennae, simple eyes, and eating. The rearbrain in the lower "neck" organizes the legs' walking movements.

MUSCLES

REAR BRAIN

POISON GLAND

ANATOMY *AT WORK*
HAVE A NICE TRIP!
A centipede runs very, very fast, yet it rarely trips over its own feet – why? The whole body curves from side to side, like a "wave." Legs on the outside of the curve lift, move forward and return to the ground, while legs on the inside stay put.

FANGS
The first pair of limbs are long, clawed, and fanglike. They jab and tear the prey and inject poison. Then the jawlike mouthparts chop up the paralyzed victim.

21

CHAPTER THREE

LOOKING INSIDE A CREATURE, there's one key feature to identify. It separates two great animal groups, invertebrates and vertebrates (see page 8). It is...vertebrae! Also called the vertebral column, spine, or backbone, it's a row of linked bones along the animal's body. It provides a strong yet flexible central support for muscle attachments and movement. Fish, amphibians, reptiles, birds, and mammals all have one.

SPIKY SPINE
The vertebral, or spinal, column has many small units, vertebrae, linked as a chain. Each vertebra has rods, spikes, and projections, where muscles are attached.

22

THE FISH'S BLOOD SYSTEM
Blood flows from the heart, along the main blood vessel to the gills. Here, it takes in oxygen, and is sent around the body. The blood, now low in oxygen, then flows back along the main veins to the heart, to be pumped back again to the gills.

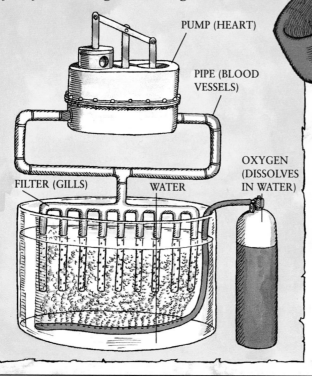

PUMP (HEART)

PIPE (BLOOD VESSELS)

OXYGEN (DISSOLVES IN WATER)

FILTER (GILLS)   WATER

GAPING GILLS
These are "underwater lungs." As the fish swims, water flows over them. Oxygen dissolved in the water passes into the blood inside the gills. The blood carries the oxygen to all body parts.

FINS AND SCALES

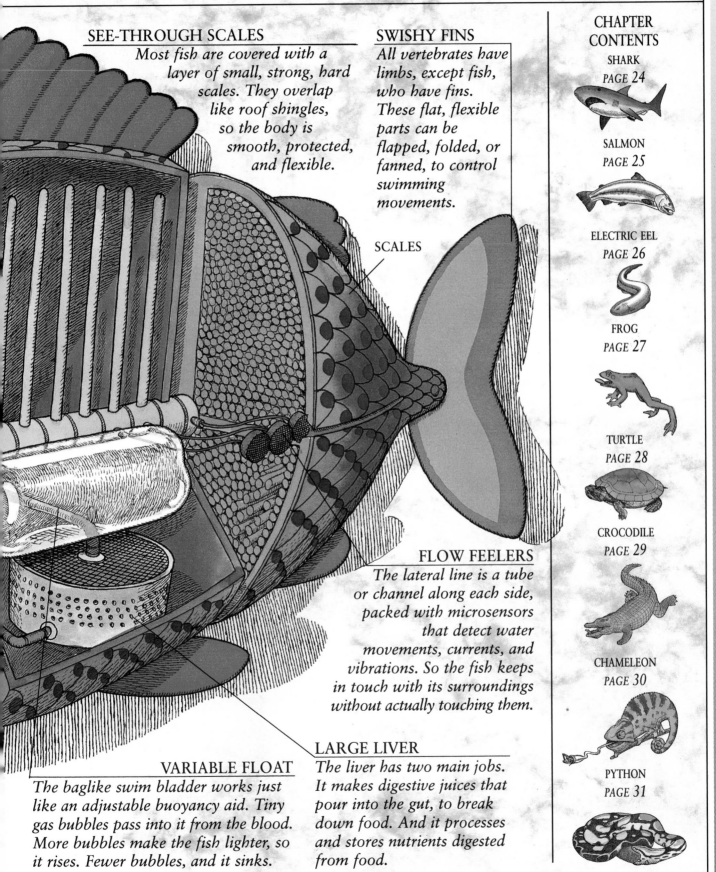

SEE-THROUGH SCALES
Most fish are covered with a layer of small, strong, hard scales. They overlap like roof shingles, so the body is smooth, protected, and flexible.

SWISHY FINS
All vertebrates have limbs, except fish, who have fins. These flat, flexible parts can be flapped, folded, or fanned, to control swimming movements.

SCALES

FLOW FEELERS
The lateral line is a tube or channel along each side, packed with microsensors that detect water movements, currents, and vibrations. So the fish keeps in touch with its surroundings without actually touching them.

VARIABLE FLOAT
The baglike swim bladder works just like an adjustable buoyancy aid. Tiny gas bubbles pass into it from the blood. More bubbles make the fish lighter, so it rises. Fewer bubbles, and it sinks.

LARGE LIVER
The liver has two main jobs. It makes digestive juices that pour into the gut, to break down food. And it processes and stores nutrients digested from food.

CHAPTER CONTENTS

SHARK
PAGE 24

SALMON
PAGE 25

ELECTRIC EEL
PAGE 26

FROG
PAGE 27

TURTLE
PAGE 28

CROCODILE
PAGE 29

CHAMELEON
PAGE 30

PYTHON
PAGE 31

23

SHARK

A SHARK IS A VERTEBRATE, but it doesn't have a backbone, or any bones at all. It has a skeleton, of course, like any other fish. But this is made of cartilage, or gristle. The flattened fish called rays also have a cartilage skeleton. Together, sharks and rays make up the cartilaginous fish group.

STURDY CARTILAGE
Compared to bone, cartilage is slightly squishy and flexible, yet still durable. It is also very light, helping to save body weight.

24

JAWS
Sharks have sharp teeth in their mouths – obviously. But their skin is also covered with tiny, teethlike points, called denticles.

GILL SLITS
Like other fish, a shark takes water into its mouth and passes it over the gills, which absorb dissolved oxygen.

LIGHT LIVER
Sharks lack a swim bladder. This problem is partly helped by the lightweight skeleton, and also by a huge liver. This contains lots of lighter-than-water oil, to give buoyancy.

SCREW GUTS
A shark's guts are relatively short and straight. But they have a large surface area for absorbing digested food, due to the screw-shaped spiral valve inside.

ANATOMY AT WORK
TOTAL TOOTH REPLACEMENT

Sharks never need a dentist. They always have new teeth. These begin on the inner sides of the jaws, and gradually grow and move forward, to the front edges. As the shark bites and feeds, they break or snap off. But more continually grow. And more...

IT WASN'T ME, HONEST!
There are about 370 different kinds of sharks. Only 20 or so attack humans regularly. They include the great white, tiger, mako, and hammerhead. Some sharklike bites may be caused by fish such as barracudas.

SALMON

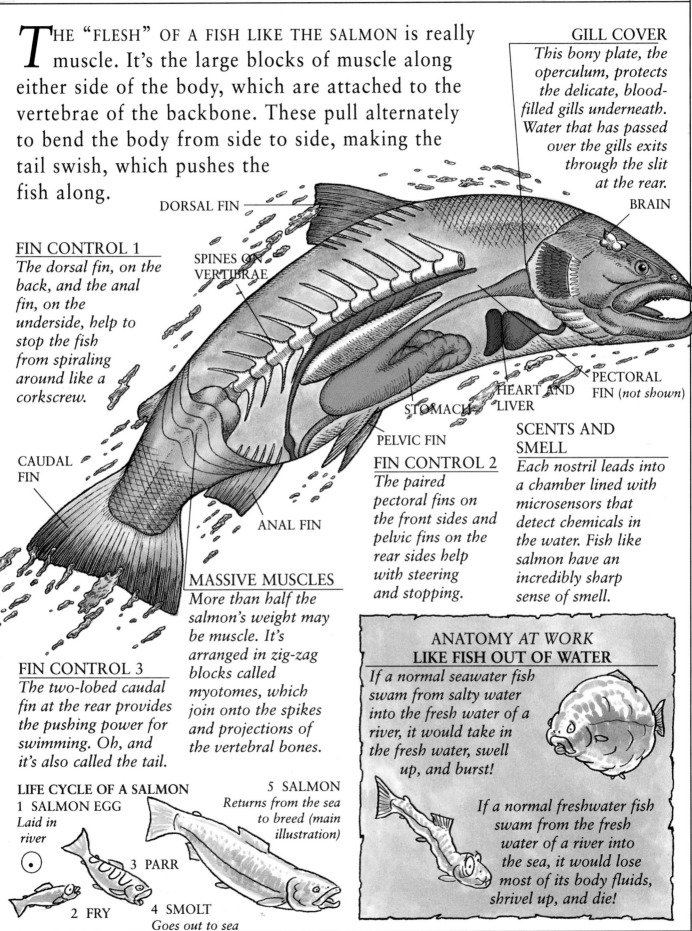

THE "FLESH" OF A FISH LIKE THE SALMON is really muscle. It's the large blocks of muscle along either side of the body, which are attached to the vertebrae of the backbone. These pull alternately to bend the body from side to side, making the tail swish, which pushes the fish along.

GILL COVER
This bony plate, the operculum, protects the delicate, blood-filled gills underneath. Water that has passed over the gills exits through the slit at the rear.

DORSAL FIN

BRAIN

FIN CONTROL 1
The dorsal fin, on the back, and the anal fin, on the underside, help to stop the fish from spiraling around like a corkscrew.

SPINES ON VERTIBRAE

HEART AND LIVER

PECTORAL FIN (*not shown*)

STOMACH

SCENTS AND SMELL
Each nostril leads into a chamber lined with microsensors that detect chemicals in the water. Fish like salmon have an incredibly sharp sense of smell.

CAUDAL FIN

PELVIC FIN

FIN CONTROL 2
The paired pectoral fins on the front sides and pelvic fins on the rear sides help with steering and stopping.

ANAL FIN

MASSIVE MUSCLES
More than half the salmon's weight may be muscle. It's arranged in zig-zag blocks called myotomes, which join onto the spikes and projections of the vertebral bones.

FIN CONTROL 3
The two-lobed caudal fin at the rear provides the pushing power for swimming. Oh, and it's also called the tail.

25

**ANATOMY *AT WORK*
LIKE FISH OUT OF WATER**
If a normal seawater fish swam from salty water into the fresh water of a river, it would take in the fresh water, swell up, and burst!

If a normal freshwater fish swam from the fresh water of a river into the sea, it would lose most of its body fluids, shrivel up, and die!

LIFE CYCLE OF A SALMON
1 SALMON EGG
Laid in river

5 SALMON
Returns from the sea to breed (main illustration)

3 PARR

2 FRY

4 SMOLT
Goes out to sea

ELECTRIC EEL

THERE ARE MANY STRANGE SHAPES and designs of fish. Some of the most curious are eels. They are almost all tail, like a swimming snake. The electric eel has a shocking surprise, too – it's not an eel! It's an eel-shaped South American gymnotid, related to the carp family.

RIGHT WAY AROUND
The electric eel has a positive and negative end, just like a battery. The head is positive, the tail is negative. But another shocking fish, the electric catfish, is the other way around.

MOSTLY TAIL
More than three quarters of an electric eel's body is its tail. This contains specialized muscle blocks that produce pulses of electricity, which the surrounding water carries very well.

LONG FIN
The electric eel has only three fins – two tiny pectorals, and one anal fin all along the underside, which it ripples to swim slowly.

SEARCH-AND-STUN
The electric eel sends out low-voltage pulses, which it also detects. Variations indicate nearby objects, like a small fish, frog, or other victim.

MUSCLES

MOUTH-LUNG
The warm, shallow Amazonian swamps where this fish lives are poor in oxygen. So it gulps air and absorbs the oxygen into rich blood vessels in the mouth lining.

SWIM BLADDER

ELECTRIC ORGAN

SMALL BODY
The inner organs, like the heart and guts, are packed into a small area at the lower front of the body.

GILLS

26

ANATOMY *AT WORK*
EEL-LECTRICITY

The electric eel has about 6,000 segments of modified muscle in its tail. They produce high-power pulses of 600 volts, each lasting 1/500th of a second. The shocks kill small animals, and stun bigger ones.

FROG

A FROG BEGINS LIFE as a water-dwelling tadpole, with gills for breathing. It grows into a mainly land-dwelling adult, with lungs for breathing. It is an amphibian (having "two lives"). Toads, salamanders, and newts are amphibians too.

BACKBONE
Like all vertebrates, frogs have a backbone. But this is one of the shortest and stiffest of all, due to the frog's jumping way of life. It has only nine vertebrae.

BRAIN   EAR

LUNGS
More than 350 million years ago, amphibians were the first vertebrates to live on land, walk on legs, and breathe air into lungs. The frog can also take in oxygen through its moist skin.

MUSCLES

BUCCAL BREATHING
Some frogs have balloonlike chins that expand and then deflate. This helps to move fresh air into the lungs, and stale air out. It's called buccal breathing.

GUT

HEART
The amphibian heart has three chambers. The left atrium receives high-oxygen blood from the lungs. The right atrium receives low-oxygen blood from the body. Both lead into the muscle-walled ventricle, which pumps the blood to the body and lungs.

LEGS
Fish have fins. Frogs and the rest of the vertebrates have limbs, usually four legs. The frog's rear pair are long and strong, with powerful muscles for leaping from danger.

27

ANATOMY *AT WORK*
HOW MANY ANIMALS?

FROG
(main illustration)

One – a frog. But it changes body shape drastically as it grows, and moves from water to land. This change in body form, both outside and within, is called metamorphosis.

EGG
Black spot surrounded by protective jelly.

YOUNG TADPOLE
Long tail for swimming. Feathery gills on the side of the head for breathing underwater.

OLDER TADPOLE
Back legs for swimming. Developing lungs for breathing air.

FROGLET
Back and front legs for leaping. Shrinking tail.

TURTLE

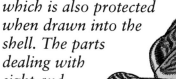

A MPHIBIANS LIKE FROGS must return to water to breed. Their eggs are soft and jelly-coated, and soon dry out on land. Reptile eggs don't. They have tough waterproof shells, so they can spend all their lives on land. Except those who choose to live in water, like the turtle.

SHELL
This has two layers. On the outside are thin, light, scutes – curved plates made of horn (keratin). Underneath are thicker, heavier osteoderms – or plates of bone.

BRAIN IN TWO BOXES
The brain is well protected inside the thick, bony skull, which is also protected when drawn into the shell. The parts dealing with sight and smell are well developed.

BEAK
Turtles and tortoises lack teeth. They bite with the hard, sharp jaw edges. They cannot chew properly either, so food often falls out before it's been swallowed.

LUNGS
These are under the highest domed part of the shell. Some turtles can hold their breath and survive underwater for more than two hours.

BODY ARMOR
For extra strength, the scutes and osteoderms (see left) are different sizes and patterns so their joints overlap.

STOMACH

BLADDER

HEART

GUTS
A plant-eating turtle has an intestine seven times longer than its body. It is coiled into the dome of the shell.

SKELETON
The main part of the backbone is joined to the underside of the upper shell. So are some of the upper limb bones, and the ribs.

HELLO, GORGEOUS
Turtles have good eyesight for finding prey and mates. But sometimes unnatural, human-made objects which are designed for the same purpose – protection – can trick them.

ANATOMY *AT WORK*
HOW THE TURTLE HIDES

A turtle's legs are longer than they seem. The upper parts, or thighs, are hidden in the shell, with space around each. A turtle in danger folds its legs, neck, and tail into these spaces. It also breathes out to make its lungs and body smaller, giving extra legroom.

28

CROCODILE

REPTILES INCLUDE TURTLES AND TORTOISES, snakes and lizards, alligators, and crocodiles. The croc's gappy "smile" means death for its prey, since its bite is one of the most powerful in the animal kingdom. It drags land animals underwater, for death by drowning.

TWO-SPEED SWIM
A croc swims quickly by sweeping its tall, narrow tail from side to side, while holding its legs against its body. It swims slowly by kicking with its rear webbed feet, using its tail to steer.

SKIN AND SKELETON
The skin has horny plates, or scutes, on it, and bony plate, or osteoderms, in it. The bones of the skeleton are strong and heavy, pulled by powerful muscles.

GUTS
(INTESTINE)

LUNGS

WINDPIPE
This tube, called the trachea, carries air into the lungs when breathing. After the oxygen is absorbed into the blood, the stale air comes back out along it.

BRAIN

BONES

BABY!

BIG BELLY
The stomach is very stretchy. It can expand to hold most of an antelope. The croc often swallows stones, which help to steady it...and may also aid digestion!

LIVER

WINDPIPE

HEART

CLOSED TO DIVE
The crocodile heart has four nearly separate chambers, almost like a mammal's (see page 38). When it dives, a flap inside diverts low-oxygen blood to the less-vital guts and other inner organs. The important brain and heart continue to receive oxygen-rich blood.

ANATOMY *AT WORK*
COLD BLOOD?
Animals like reptiles are sometimes called "cold-blooded." Mammals are warm-blooded (see page 38). But a crocodile basking in the sun may have blood hotter than yours! They control body temperature by basking in the sun or cooling off in the shade.

CHAMELEON

L IZARDS DON'T GET MUCH stranger than the chameleon. This tall-backed, flat-sided tree-dweller moves incredibly slowly, or not at all, as it stalks small animals like insects, baby birds, and mice.

LOTS OF BACKBONE
A long lizard may have more than 200 vertebrae, which extend to its tail-tip. This compares to your 26 vertebrae.

NERVES

SCALES
The scales are made of the lightweight substance keratin (horn). They protect, allow movement, and also reduce fluid loss, which is why many kinds of lizards can live in the driest deserts.

HEART

SCHLUUUP!
The long tongue is almost entirely muscle. It is flicked out at lightning speed to catch small creatures on its sticky tip.

GLOSSAL BONE

TONGUE MUSCLE

HOOKED FEET
The toes face each other, making a hook shape for gripping twigs.

FIFTH FOOT
The tail is prehensile – its muscles pull the backbones within it into a curly shape to grip branches like a fifth foot.

30

ANATOMY *AT* WORK
TWO VIEWS ON LIFE
A chameleon's eyes are like cone-shaped turrets. They can swivel to see all around, and even look in different directions, at different things. Exactly what the chameleon does with the two views, in its brain, is a mystery!

TOO DIFFICULT?!
Chameleons change their skin colors to blend in with different surroundings. They do this by clumping together or spreading out tiny particles inside the microscopic cells in their skin. But some of our artificial patterns are too difficult!

PYTHON

DURING EVOLUTION and the struggle for survival, snakes like the python have lost – body parts, that is. They include parts such as legs and most of one lung. But never mind – the long, slim, snaky shape is ideal for burrowing in loose soil, swimming, climbing, or simply slithering along the ground.

ALL TIED UP

A snake is, in effect, one long set of backbones. Some species have nearly 400 vertebrae! Muscles along the sides bend the body around and back again. A snake can tie itself in knots, but it can easily undo them.

STRAIGHT GUTS

A snake is much the same shape as its intestines, which do not have to be folded and coiled.

STAGGERED KIDNEYS

In vertebrates, two kidneys filter unwanted substances from the blood. In snakes the kidneys are staggered, one behind the other. Side by side, they'd make a wide bulge!

STOMACH

LIVER

LUNGS

31

RIBS

BACKBONE

HEART

KIDNEYS

NO LEGS

Pythons and boas have two tiny "claws" under the tail, on either side. They are all that's left of the four limbs of other reptiles. Other snakes lack even these claws.

ONE LUNG

Instead of two lungs side by side, a snake has only one main lung – the right. It is long and is wrapped around the windpipe, for extra oxygen-absorbing capacity.

SNAKE SNACK

Snakes cannot chew, but they can swallow victims wider than their heads! This is done by stretching the joints between the jaw bones, to make the mouth wider and higher.

ANATOMY AT WORK
SNIFFING WITH THE TONGUE

Why does a snake flick its tongue? When out, it gathers smell particles from the air. It pushes these into an extra "nose," Jacobson's organ in the roof of the mouth, which detects the particles.

CHAPTER FOUR

VARIOUS ANIMALS CAN GLIDE, from squirrels and possums to snakes and lizards. But only insects, bats, and birds can truly fly. To be a good flier, you need a very light body. Birds have lots of weight-saving features, like no heavy teeth, hollow bones, and a body covering that's as light as...feathers. Oh, and wings are helpful, too!

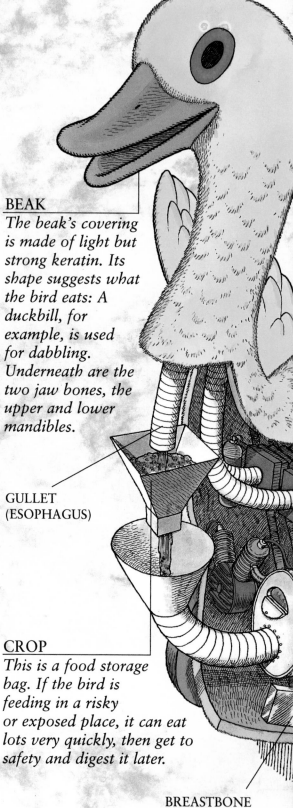

BEAK
The beak's covering is made of light but strong keratin. Its shape suggests what the bird eats: A duckbill, for example, is used for dabbling. Underneath are the two jaw bones, the upper and lower mandibles.

GULLET (ESOPHAGUS)

CROP
This is a food storage bag. If the bird is feeding in a risky or exposed place, it can eat lots very quickly, then get to safety and digest it later.

BREASTBONE (STERNUM)

ALL ABOUT FEATHERS

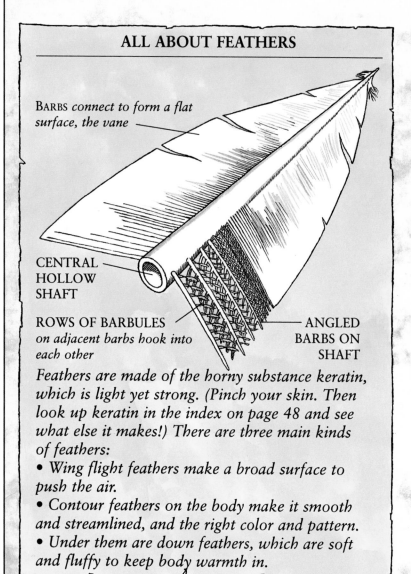

BARBS *connect to form a flat surface, the vane*

CENTRAL HOLLOW SHAFT

ROWS OF BARBULES *on adjacent barbs hook into each other*

ANGLED BARBS ON SHAFT

Feathers are made of the horny substance keratin, which is light yet strong. (Pinch your skin. Then look up keratin in the index on page 48 and see what else it makes!) There are three main kinds of feathers:
• *Wing flight feathers make a broad surface to push the air.*
• *Contour feathers on the body make it smooth and streamlined, and the right color and pattern.*
• *Under them are down feathers, which are soft and fluffy to keep body warmth in.*

FEATHERED FRIENDS

LUNGS

A bird is usually very active, so it needs lots of oxygen. Bird lungs are relatively big, with lots of blood to take up oxygen. To make them more efficient, air flows right through them, back and forth, to air sacs beyond.

WINGS

These are front limbs which have changed their job, during evolution, from walking to flapping. Their skeletons are much the same as any vertebrate limb, except the wrist and finger bones are much smaller (see page 36).

EGG FROM OVIDUCT WHERE IT RECEIVED YOLK AND SHELL

EGGS

A bird turns some of its food into energy and nutrients for its own busy, active, warm-blooded body. The rest is turned into baby birds, well protected inside their strong eggshells.

EGGS EMERGE THROUGH CLOACA

WHEELS?

No, not really. A bird's rear limbs are fairly ordinary legs, as shown on the next pages.

CHAPTER CONTENTS

OSTRICH
PAGE 34

PENGUIN
PAGE 35

SWALLOW
PAGE 36

OWL
PAGE 37

33

THE BIRD'S HEART

The bird heart is much the same as the mammalian heart (see the mammal's heart, page 39).

OSTRICH

THE BIGGEST BIRDS ARE THE OSTRICH from Africa, the emu from Australia, and the rhea from South America. They are too heavy to fly. But these flightless birds, called ratites (pronounced ray-teetz), are suited to life walking and running on the ground.

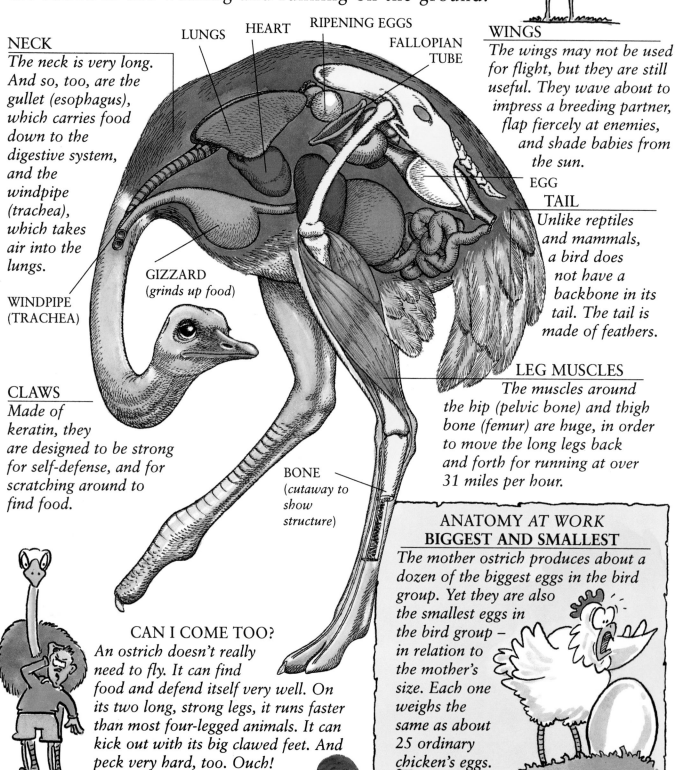

NECK
The neck is very long. And so, too, are the gullet (esophagus), which carries food down to the digestive system, and the windpipe (trachea), which takes air into the lungs.

WINDPIPE (TRACHEA)

GIZZARD
(grinds up food)

LUNGS HEART RIPENING EGGS FALLOPIAN TUBE

WINGS
The wings may not be used for flight, but they are still useful. They wave about to impress a breeding partner, flap fiercely at enemies, and shade babies from the sun.

EGG

TAIL
Unlike reptiles and mammals, a bird does not have a backbone in its tail. The tail is made of feathers.

CLAWS
Made of keratin, they are designed to be strong for self-defense, and for scratching around to find food.

BONE
(cutaway to show structure)

LEG MUSCLES
The muscles around the hip (pelvic bone) and thigh bone (femur) are huge, in order to move the long legs back and forth for running at over 31 miles per hour.

CAN I COME TOO?
An ostrich doesn't really need to fly. It can find food and defend itself very well. On its two long, strong legs, it runs faster than most four-legged animals. It can kick out with its big clawed feet. And peck very hard, too. Ouch!

ANATOMY *AT* WORK
BIGGEST AND SMALLEST
The mother ostrich produces about a dozen of the biggest eggs in the bird group. Yet they are also the smallest eggs in the bird group – in relation to the mother's size. Each one weighs the same as about 25 ordinary chicken's eggs.

PENGUIN

PENGUINS ARE DESIGNED FOR LIFE in cold seas. Their flipper-shaped wings and webbed feet are ideal for swimming. And they are never troubled by polar bears because penguins live in the South Atlantic Ocean and Antarctica, while polar bears live at the other end of the world, in the Arctic north.

FLAPSTROKE, NOT BACKSTROKE

Penguins can fly – Not in the air, but through water. They flap their flipperlike wings up and down, just like any other flying bird, and speed along faster than any human swimmer. However, they cannot do the backstroke.

COLD FEET

The feet and flippers are designed to be cold. As blood from the warm central body goes into them, it flows next to cooler blood coming back, and is cooled. This reduces heat loss from feet and flippers into the sea, while the returning blood is warmed.

ARTERIES (red)

VEINS (purple)

BONES

MUSCLES

FAT IS FINE

The penguin's stout, body has a thick layer of the fatty substance, blubber, just beneath the skin. This helps to keep the cold out. It also makes the body's outline smoother and more streamlined, for swimming.

DOWN, DROWN

Like any bird, a penguin needs to breathe fresh air regularly into its lungs. If it is kept underwater for more than a few minutes, it drowns.

AIR SACS

WINDPIPE (TRACHEA)

SNAPPER

The strong, stout, sharp-edged beak is ideal for snapping and catching prey such as slippery fish and squid, and hard-cased shellfish.

35

ANATOMY AT WORK
STOMACH

After the mouth, gullet, and crop, the next part of a bird's gut is the gizzard, or stomach. This has very thick, muscular walls. Birds cannot chew, so it's the gizzard's job to grind up food.

SALT GLANDS
(for ridding the blood of excess salt)

SWALLOW

O N THE WING FROM DAWN TO DUSK, few birds fly more hours than the swallow. And swallow it does, as it snaps at tiny flying insects such as gnats and midges. It must eat thousands daily to get enough energy for all that flying and to store food in its body for the long journey south each fall, to warmer tropical places where it spends the winter.

WING SHAPE
The swallow's curved, crescent-shaped wings show a fast and aerobatic flier. Birds with long, straight, narrow wings, like gulls, tend to glide and soar more.

FEATHER FIXINGS
The root of each feather shaft is joined to tendons (that connect to the muscles) in the thick skin. Thin muscles tilt and fan the feathers for aerobatic control.

WING BONES
The upper-arm and forearm bones are much the same as other four-limbed vertebrates. But the wrist bones are small, and the fingers are tiny, with two completely missing.

36

LUNGS

AIR SACS

TAIL FEATHERS
(*called* RECTRICES)

PECTORAL
MUSCLES

LIGHT
SNACK

WINDPIPE
(TRACHEA)

KEEL
This is a large flap, or flange, on the breastbone (sternum). It anchors the inner ends of the flight muscles. The bigger it is, the better the bird flies.

BODY ORGANS
Birds have all the usual vertebrate body parts: kidneys to filter wastes from the blood, a pancreas to make digestive juices, and a liver to do this too (as well as store and process nutrients).

z z z z z z z z z z z z z z z z z Z Z Z Z

Swallows rest and doze on the wing, and even mate in midair.

ANATOMY *AT WORK*
HOW BIRDS FLY

1 PECTORALIS MINOR MUSCLE (*pulls wing up*)

2 PECTORALIS MAJOR MUSCLE

The main force for flight comes from the pectoralis major muscle on either side of the bird's breast. This pulls the upper arm bone, which flaps the whole wing downward and backward. It pushes air down and back too, and thrusts the bird upward and forward.

OWL

TWIT, TWOO. Hoot, hoot. Whooooo! Owl calls echo eerily in the silent night. This hunting bird swoops as quietly as a ghost, too. The victim, a wood rat, knows nothing until the owl's hard, curved claws spear its body and carry it away into the darkness. Gulp! Frightening!

EEK!

ANATOMY *AT WORK*
UGH, CUCK, GUG, CAG...COUGH!
Hard bits of an owl's food, like bones, teeth, claws, skin, insect wing-covers, and fish scales, are difficult to digest. In the gizzard, the remains are pressed into a pellet, which the owl regurgitates (brings up) a few hours later.

NIGHT SIGHT
An owl's eyes fill more than half its skull. They gather as much light as possible for hunting in almost complete darkness. Even with computer-aided, night-vision binoculars, we cannot see as well as an owl.

BIRD BRAIN
Compared to most other animals, birds have relatively big brains. The parts dealing with sight (optic lobes) and movement coordination (cerebellum) are especially large.

37

LUNGS

BONES

MUSCLES

STOMACH

KEEL

HOOKED BEAK
The strong, curved beak, or bill, is designed for ripping and tearing small animals, which are held by the claws or talons. Claws and beaks are made of...? (Guess.)

LUNCH
An owl eats meat, which is easily digestible and nutritious. So its intestines are relatively small and short. A bird like a pigeon, which eats lots of much-less-nutritious plant food, has an intestine up to five times longer.

NOT KNEE
The bird's equivalent of the knee joint is very near the body, usually hidden by feathers. What looks like its "knee" is really its ankle.

TENDONS

CHAPTER *FIVE*

CUDDLY. FURRY. WARMY. BABY. MILKY. Four of these are key features of all mammals. (Find the odd one out below.) All mammals have fur or hair. Even super-smooth whales and dolphins have a tiny bit. Mammals are warm-blooded, keeping a constant body temperature. Female mammals give birth to babies, rather than laying eggs. And mammal mothers feed their babies on their own milk. (The odd one out was "cuddly." Sperm whales and vampire bats are mammals, but THEY'RE not very cuddly!)

38

BIG BRAIN
Compared to stupid creatures like fish, mammals have big brains relative to their body size. So they're quite...er...clever.

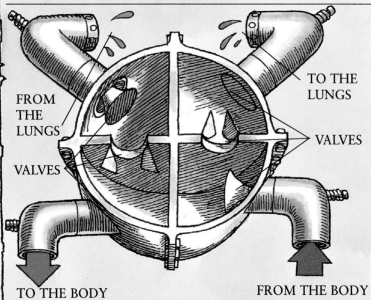

THE MAMMAL HEART

FROM THE LUNGS

TO THE LUNGS

VALVES

VALVES

TO THE BODY

FROM THE BODY

Only mammals (and birds) have a four-part heart. The two right pumping chambers send blood to the lungs, where it receives oxygen. Blood flows back to the left chambers, which send it around the body.

WARM BLOOD
Mammals make warmth in their bodies, which keeps their temperature around 95-104°F (35-40°C). Blood spreads the heat to all body parts.

MAMMALS

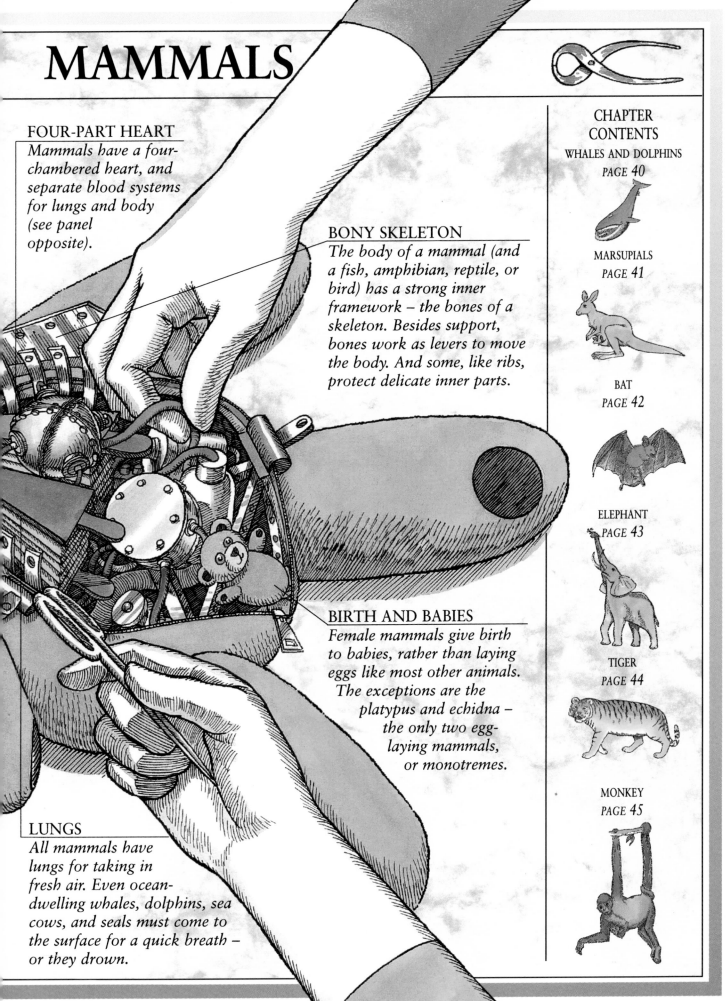

FOUR-PART HEART
Mammals have a four-chambered heart, and separate blood systems for lungs and body (see panel opposite).

BONY SKELETON
The body of a mammal (and a fish, amphibian, reptile, or bird) has a strong inner framework – the bones of a skeleton. Besides support, bones work as levers to move the body. And some, like ribs, protect delicate inner parts.

BIRTH AND BABIES
Female mammals give birth to babies, rather than laying eggs like most other animals. The exceptions are the platypus and echidna – the only two egg-laying mammals, or monotremes.

LUNGS
All mammals have lungs for taking in fresh air. Even ocean-dwelling whales, dolphins, sea cows, and seals must come to the surface for a quick breath – or they drown.

CHAPTER CONTENTS
WHALES AND DOLPHINS
PAGE 40

MARSUPIALS
PAGE 41

BAT
PAGE 42

ELEPHANT
PAGE 43

TIGER
PAGE 44

MONKEY
PAGE 45

39

WHALE

Y OU'D WIN A RUNNING RACE against a whale. But it would win at swimming. Whales and dolphins are perfectly at home in water. Their arms are flippers, their legs have disappeared, and their tails are broad flukes (see right). But the rest of a whale is much like any other mammal inside, except a lot bigger.

INTESTINES

FLAPPY FLUKES
These wide flaps of muscle and gristle give the main push for swimming.

BABY'S BIRTH
As soon as her baby is born, the mother whale nudges it to the surface for its first gasp of air.

STOMACH

LUNGS

NOSE HOLE
The whale's nose is on top of its head. It's the blowhole or nostrils, the opening for breathing air.

LIVER

HEART

40

HANDY FLIPPERS
Flippers are mainly for steering, being arms in disguise. Inside are all the usual mammal arm and hand bones.

BRAIN

SKULL

LOWER JAWBONE (MANDIBLE)

ANATOMY *AT WORK*
SO NEAR (OR FAR)

Dolphins squeak a lot and squeal, and go "kikikiki." Sometimes for fun. But these high-pitched sounds also bounce off objects, like fish or rocks. The dolphin hears the returning echoes and knows what's near. It's called sonar!

SLEEK FOR SPEED
Why is a great whale like a submarine? It's a smooth, streamlined shape for speeding through the water.

BIG MOUTH
The blue whale gulps shrimplike krill into its minivan-sized mouth. It combs them from the water with jaws of baleen, or whalebone.

DOLPHINS *are small, sharp-toothed whales*

KANGAROO

HOW CAN YOU TELL a mother marsupial? She's got a baby in her pocket. The pocket, or pouch, is called a marsupium, and marsupials like kangaroos and koalas are the only mammals with them. The marsupial baby is born in the usual way, but it is tiny, furless, blind, and almost helpless. All it can do is crawl to the pouch, where it feeds on milk and grows for many more weeks.

ANATOMY *AT WORK*

THE BIG CLIMB

The newborn kangaroo is a mini-blob, like a jellybean. But it knows how to wriggle and climb through mom's fur, from her birth opening down below, up to the safety of her pouch.

41

JUMPING POWER
Kangaroos and wallabies can't run. But they can bounce, hop, leap, and jump with their long, powerful back legs and massive feet.

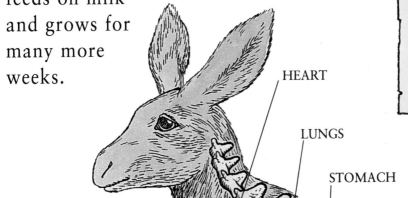

HEART

LUNGS

STOMACH

MUSCLE

YOU CAN'T GET ME
After six months, the young kangaroo, or joey, is big enough to leave the pouch and hop around on its own. But if it's still thirsty for milk, or if danger appears, it leaps back in.

BIT OF BALANCE
The kangaroo's long, thick, heavy tail balances its body, as it "boings" along. It's also good for whacking enemies.

SKELETON IN TAIL

FEMUR (THIGH BONE)

WOMBAT

KOALA

MARSUPIAL MENAGERIE
There are about 260 kinds of marsupials, from huge 'roos to cat-sized tasmanian devils, wombats, and cuddly koalas.

BABY ON THE WAY
This mother's joey will soon leave. But already, there's another baby developing in her womb.

TASMANIAN DEVIL

BAT

THERE ARE ABOUT 4,000 KINDS, or species, of mammals. About 900 – nearly one quarter – are bats. But we don't often see them, for three reasons. Most bats are active at night, when we aren't. Most bats find their way in the dark, which we can't. And most live in dense tropical forests, where we don't.

42

BAT NAPPING
Bats rest upside-down in sheltered places like caves, tree holes, barns, and roofs, called roosts. The hanging body weight makes the long, stringlike tendons in the feet pull the claws into a hooked position. So as the bat falls asleep, it doesn't fall off its roost!

EARS
A bat can turn and swivel its large ears like satellite dishes, to catch the returning echoes of its ultrasound squeaks.

WING
Over millions of years of evolution, the bat's arms have become wings. The wing membrane, the patagium, is an amazingly thin sandwich of two skin layers with muscle fibers between. It's light and flexible, yet strong.

BRAIN

LUNGS

FINGER BONE

ARM BONES
The bones of the four fingers are long and thin, in order to hold out the wing. The thumb is a small claw. It's used for crawling around the roost and gripping food.

WINDPIPE (TRACHEA)

DINNER

MUSCLES
Pectoral chest muscles provide the power to flap the wings. Like a bird, the bat's body is small and very lightweight.

NOSE OR MOUTH?
Some bats send out their high-pitched sounds through the mouth. Others, like the horseshoe and leaf-nosed bats, beam them through the nose!

ANATOMY *AT* WORK
HUNTING BY HEARING

In the dark night, a bat finds its way and prey by sound (like a dolphin, see page 40). It makes clicks, beeps, and squeaks, which are ultrasonic (too high for most people to hear). These bounce off nearby objects as echoes. From the echoes' patterns, the bat works out the object's size, shape, and movement.

ELEPHANT

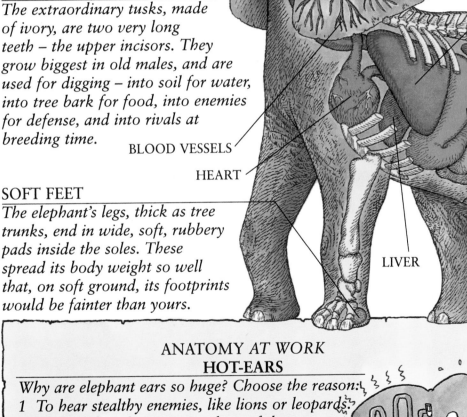

USEFUL TRUNK
The upper lip and nose have become the long, flexible trunk. It's used for feeding, smelling, stroking herd members, and for sucking up water to squirt into the mouth when drinking or over the back to keep cool. But not for packing clothes to go on vacation!

T HE ELEPHANT IS THE WORLD'S LARGEST mammal. No, sorry...the blue whale is. An elephant is the largest land mammal. A large bull, or male, elephant can weigh six tons. A cow, or female, elephant is about half this. (And a blue whale is twenty times this.)

TUSKS
The extraordinary tusks, made of ivory, are two very long teeth – the upper incisors. They grow biggest in old males, and are used for digging – into soil for water, into tree bark for food, into enemies for defense, and into rivals at breeding time.

BLOOD VESSELS

HEART

SOFT FEET
The elephant's legs, thick as tree trunks, end in wide, soft, rubbery pads inside the soles. These spread its body weight so well that, on soft ground, its footprints would be fainter than yours.

SKULL
An elephant's skull has lots of tiny air holes, like a sponge. Yet it is so enormous that it's still one fifth the weight of the whole skeleton.

LUNG
BACKBONE
KIDNEY
OVARY
INTESTINES (GUTS)
PELVIS (HIP BONE)

43

LIVER

SKIN
It's thicker than your thumb!

STOMACH
The enormous stomach is bigger than a household garbage can. Another part of the gut, the cecum, is the same size. Elephants eat 300 pounds (150 kilos) of food daily – over 100 times more than you.

ANATOMY AT WORK
HOT-EARS
Why are elephant ears so huge? Choose the reason:
1 To hear stealthy enemies, like lions or leopards.
2 To hear friends, since members of the herd "talk" using infrasonic (very deep) rumbling sounds.
3 To stay cool by flapping them. In the scorching tropical heat, big ears work like radiators and get rid of excess body warmth.
Answer: All three, of course!

TIGER

S UPERBLY DESIGNED FOR NIGHTTIME HUNTING, the tiger is the biggest member of the cat family. It rarely runs far. Instead it stalks stealthily, then stages a short sprint, and silently springs on the victim. Yet inside, it's just a twenty-times-bigger version of a pet cat.

EYES
Huge eyes for seeing in dim light show that cats are not diurnal (day-active), but nocturnal (night-active). Well, really they are more crepuscular, hunting in the twilight of dusk and dawn.

LUNGS
Nothing special here. Cats, like all mammals, have two lungs for absorbing oxygen from the air.

KIDNEY

SCENT-SPRAY
The cat sprays its stinky urine and smears smelly anal gland fluid on tree-trunks and rocks. To other cats, the odors mean: "Stay away, this is my territory."

INTESTINES

44

TEETH
Daggerlike canine front teeth grab and spear prey. Shearlike carnassial cheek teeth slice flesh and crush bone.

CLAW

HEART

LIVER

STOMACH

FOREARM BONES

TENDON

CUBS

BLADDER *(for waste urine)*

TOP CAT'S FAMILY
There are around 35 kinds of cats. Biggest is the tiger. Other big cats are the lion, leopard, cheetah, and jaguar. Smallest is the black-footed cat of Africa. It's about the same size as a pet cat.

ANATOMY *AT WORK*
CLAW WITHDRAW
Dog claws stick out of the toes all the time, and get worn and blunt. Cat claws are usually retracted. Hingelike toe joints are bent, to keep the claws sharp in protective sheaths at the toe ends. To unretract, the cat contracts muscles to straighten the toe joints.

TAIL
A cat's vertebrae (backbones) extend all the way to its tail-tip, and are moved by slim muscles. The tail helps balance when climbing, and is swished and switched to show mood and intent.

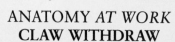

MONKEY

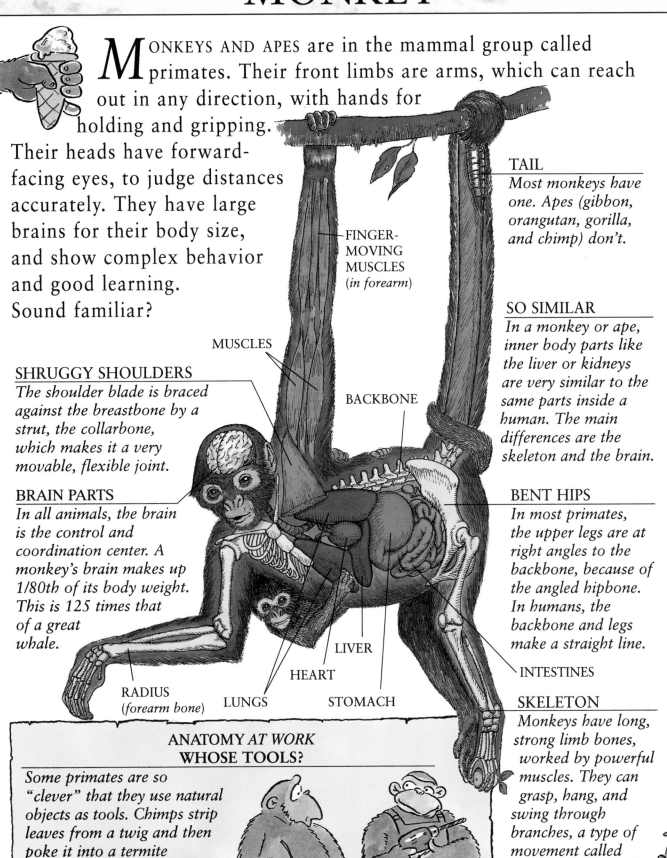

MONKEYS AND APES are in the mammal group called primates. Their front limbs are arms, which can reach out in any direction, with hands for holding and gripping. Their heads have forward-facing eyes, to judge distances accurately. They have large brains for their body size, and show complex behavior and good learning. Sound familiar?

FINGER-MOVING MUSCLES
(in forearm)

TAIL
Most monkeys have one. Apes (gibbon, orangutan, gorilla, and chimp) don't.

MUSCLES

SO SIMILAR
In a monkey or ape, inner body parts like the liver or kidneys are very similar to the same parts inside a human. The main differences are the skeleton and the brain.

BACKBONE

SHRUGGY SHOULDERS
The shoulder blade is braced against the breastbone by a strut, the collarbone, which makes it a very movable, flexible joint.

BRAIN PARTS
In all animals, the brain is the control and coordination center. A monkey's brain makes up 1/80th of its body weight. This is 125 times that of a great whale.

BENT HIPS
In most primates, the upper legs are at right angles to the backbone, because of the angled hipbone. In humans, the backbone and legs make a straight line.

INTESTINES

RADIUS
(forearm bone)

LUNGS

HEART

LIVER

STOMACH

SKELETON
Monkeys have long, strong limb bones, worked by powerful muscles. They can grasp, hang, and swing through branches, a type of movement called brachiation.

ANATOMY *AT WORK*
WHOSE TOOLS?

Some primates are so "clever" that they use natural objects as tools. Chimps strip leaves from a twig and then poke it into a termite mound, to get out the juicy termites. But they haven't invented power tools, yet!

45

ANIMAL CLASSIFICATION

SPONGES
(Phylum Porifera)

JELLYFISH, ANEMONES, AND CORALS
(Phylum Cnidaria or Coelenterata)

EARTHWORMS AND OTHER TRUE WORMS
(Phylum Annelida)

SNAILS, SQUIDS, AND OTHER MOLLUSKS
(Phylum Mollusca)

STARFISH AND SEA URCHINS
(Phylum Echinodermata)

ARTHROPODS
(Phylum Arthropoda)
- CRABS, LOBSTERS, AND OTHER CRUSTACEANS
  (Class Crustacea)
- CENTIPEDES
  (Class Chilopoda)
- MILLIPEDES
  (Class Diplopoda)
- INSECTS
  (Class Insecta)
- SPIDERS AND SCORPIONS
  (Class Arachnida)

CHORDATES
(Phylum Chordata)
- ANIMALS WITH BACKBONES
  (Sub-phylum Vertebrata)
- SHARKS, SKATES, AND RAYS
  (Class Chondrichthyes)
- BONY FISH
  (Class Osteichthyes)
- FROGS, SALAMANDERS, AND OTHER AMPHIBIANS
  (Class Amphibia)
- CROCS, SNAKES, LIZARDS, TURTLES, AND OTHER REPTILES
  (Class Reptilia)
- BIRDS
  (Class Aves)
- MAMMALS
  (Class Mammalia)
  - Monotremes, platypus, and echidnas, who lay eggs.
  - Marsupials – kangaroos, etc.
  - Placentals – all other mammals.

SCIENTISTS GROUP animals according to their likenesses and separate them by their differences, which produces an animal classification chart like this one. Unfortunately, it tends to make the whole thing look a bit complicated. And this one shows just the animals covered in this book – a fraction of the whole animal kingdom! But in fact it's a neat and tidy way to organize information about animals, and to show how they are related to each other. So now you know!

GLOSSARY

Artery A blood vessel that takes blood away from the heart.

Bone A strong, stiff body part that, as part of a skeleton, holds up all the other soft, squishy parts.

Cartilage A firm, white, bonelike substance that forms the skeleton of sharks, rays, skates, and chimera.

Digestion The breakdown of food, and the absorption of the important parts of it into a body.

Endoskeleton A skeleton or framework found on the inside of an animal's body – like mammals and birds.

Exoskeleton A hard supporting or protective structure found on the outside of creatures like insects.

Gill A feathery body part specialized for absorbing dissolved oxygen from water.

Gizzard A muscular, thick-walled part of the digestive system, that grinds up food.

Heart A thick-walled, muscular part of the blood vessel system, which pumps blood.

Intestines (guts) Part of the system that breaks down (digests) food to remove the nutrients needed by the body.

Invertebrates Collective term for animals without backbones. They include insects, spiders, octopuses, jellyfish, worms, crabs, and starfish.

Kidneys Structures that filter blood and remove wastes.

Liver A large organ that processes chemicals in the body.

Mantle The fleshy, cloaklike body wrapping of a mollusk like a squid.

Muscle A body part specialized to get shorter, or contract, in order to move whatever it is joined to (like a bone). Many organs have their own muscles, such as the heart and intestines.

Nerve Nerves transmit signals from the sense organs (eyes, ears, and so on) to the brain, telling it about the world around.

Ovary The female reproductive organ, which makes eggs.

Oviduct Part of the reproductive system, which stores and conveys eggs.

Stomach A baglike part of the digestive system, where strong chemicals break down food.

Trachea Windpipe, which carries air into and out of the lungs.

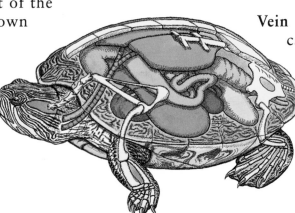

Vein A blood vessel that carries blood back to the heart.

Vertebrate Animals with backbones or the equivalent in cartilage. Fish, amphibians, reptiles, birds, and mammals are vertebrates.

INDEX

A

amphibians 27, 28
antennae 18, 19
apes 45
arachnids 20
arthropods 13,
21

B

babies 39, 40
bats 42
beaks 28, 37
bees 19
beetles 17
birds 32-37
brains 6, 9, 19,
21, 28, 37, 38, 45
butterflies 18

C

cartilage 24
caterpillars 18
cats 44
centipedes 21
chameleons 30
claws 34, 44
corals 10
crocodiles 29
crustaceans 13

D

digestion 18, 35, 37,
47
dolphins 40
dragonflies 16

E

ears 42, 43
earthworms 8-9
eggs 28, 33, 34
electric eels 26
elephants 43
emus 34

endoskeletons 7, 47
exoskeletons 7, 13,
15, 20, 47
eyes 7, 12, 16,
28, 30, 44, 45

F

feathers 7, 32, 36
fins 23, 25, 26
fishes 22-26
flies 14
flight 16, 32-33, 36
flippers 40
frogs 27

G

gills 13, 22, 24,
25, 27
guts 7, 9, 14, 19, 24,
28, 31, 47

H

hearts 6, 27,
29, 38, 39
hippos 6-7

I

insects 14-19
intestines
see guts
invertebrates 8,
22

J

jellyfish 10

K

kangaroos 41
keratin 28, 30, 32,
34, 37
kidneys 7, 31, 47

L

livers 7, 23, 24, 47
lizards 30
lobsters 13
lungs 27, 28,
31, 33, 39, 44

M

mammals 38-45
marsupials 41
metamorphosis 18, 27
migration 36
mollusks 12
monkeys 45
mosquitoes 6-7
moths 18
muscles 6, 8, 25, 34,
42

O

octopuses 12
ostriches 34
owls 37

P

penguins 35
pincers 13, 20
poison 10, 19
polyps 10
primates 45
pythons 31

R

rays 24
reptiles 28-29

S

salmon 25
scorpions 20
sharks 24
skeletons 7, 28, 39,
45
snakes 31
sonar 40
spiders 20
squid 12
starfish 11
stings 19
stomachs 10, 11, 35,
43
suckers 11, 12
swallows 36

T

tails 41, 44, 45
teeth 24, 44
tentacles 10
tigers 44
turtles 28
tusks 43

V

vertebrates 8,
22, 27

W

whales 40, 43

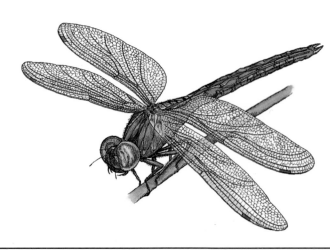